Wild Outdoors

Pheasant Hunting

by Jeanie Mebane

Reading Consultant: Barbara J. Fox
Reading Specialist
North Carolina State University

Content Consultant:
Maggie Lindsey
Education Services Coordinator
South Dakota Game, Fish, and Parks

CAPSTONE PRESS
a capstone imprint

Blazers is published by Capstone Press,
151 Good Counsel Drive, P.O. Box 669, Mankato, Minnesota 56002.
www.capstonepub.com

 Books published by Capstone Press are manufactured with paper
containing at least 10 percent post-consumer waste.

Library of Congress Cataloging-in-Publication Data
Mebane, Jeanie.
  Pheasant hunting / by Jeanie Mebane.
      p. cm. — (Blazers. Wild outdoors)
  Includes bibliographical references and index.
  Summary: "Describes the equipment, skills, and techniques needed for pheasant
hunting"—Provided by publisher.
  ISBN 978-1-4296-6005-1 (library binding)
  1. Pheasant shooting—Juvenile literature. I. Title. II. Series.
  SK325.P5M43 2012
  799.2'4625—dc22   2011003786

Editorial Credits
Angie Kaelberer, editor; Gene Bentdahl, designer; Sarah Schuette, photo stylist;
    Marcy Morin, scheduler; Eric Manske, production specialist

Photo Credits
Alamy: Daniel Dempster Photography, 18–19, 26–27; AP Images: Hays Daily News/Steven
Hausler, 29, The Hutchinson News/Travis Morisse, 10–11; Capstone Studio: Karon Dubke,
14–15; iStockphoto: Jason Lugo, cover, 5, 6–7, 12–13 (all), 24–25; Newscom/MCT: Brad
Dokken, 8–9, Paul A. Smith, 11 (front), Sam Cook, 22–23; Shutterstock: Linn Currie, 16–17,
NanoStock, 20–21, Peter Wollinga, 6 (front)

Artistic Effects
Capstone Studio: Karon Dubke (woods); Shutterstock: rvika (wood), rvrspb (fence),
VikaSuh (sign)

Printed in the United States of America in Stevens Point, Wisconsin.
032011   006111WZF11

Table of Contents

Chapter 1
A Good Day for a Hunt

You walk near a creek on a sunny fall morning. Ahead you see a flash of green, white, and brown feathers through the **brush**. It's a pheasant!

brush—a thick growth of shrubs and small trees close to the ground

Wild Fact:

Pheasants were brought to North America from China more than 100 years ago.

The pheasant rises into the air.
You lift your shotgun, aim, and fire.
The bird drops to the ground.

Wild Fact:

Pheasants can be 35 inches (89 centimeters) long. They weigh 2 to 3 pounds (0.9 to 1.4 kilograms).

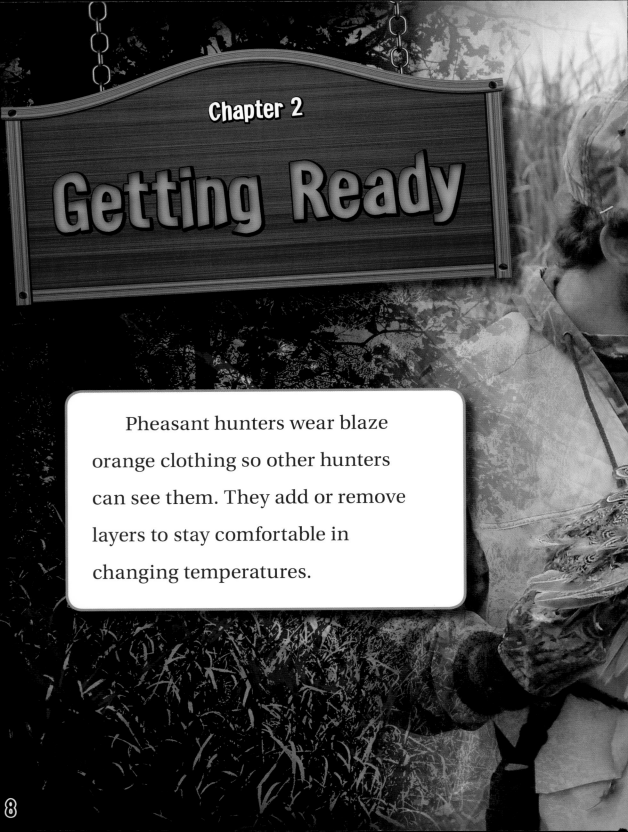

Chapter 2
Getting Ready

Pheasant hunters wear blaze orange clothing so other hunters can see them. They add or remove layers to stay comfortable in changing temperatures.

Wild Fact:

Many hunters wear brush pants covered with material that doesn't catch on brush.

Many states require young hunters to hunt with an adult. States also limit the number of birds hunters can shoot and the days they can hunt.

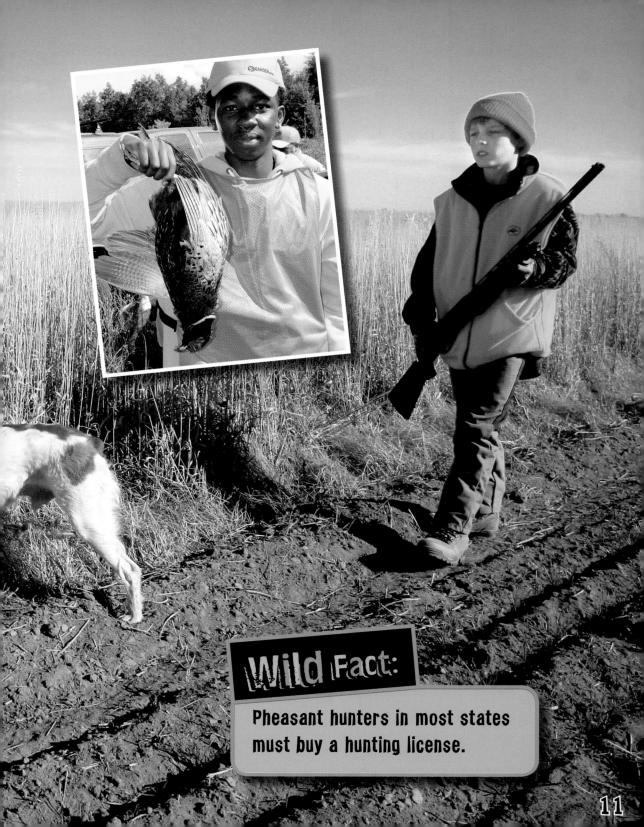

Pheasant hunters in most states must buy a hunting license.

Pheasant hunters use shotguns. These guns fire a wide spray of **shot**, which makes hitting flying targets easier. Shotguns can hit pheasants up to 150 feet (46 meters) away.

shot—small metal beads or pellets

Wild Fact:

Young hunters usually use shotguns weighing less than 8 pounds (3.6 kg).

Pheasant Hunting Equipment

warm
hat

shell
vest

hunting dog

boots

hunting
license

compass

GPS

maps

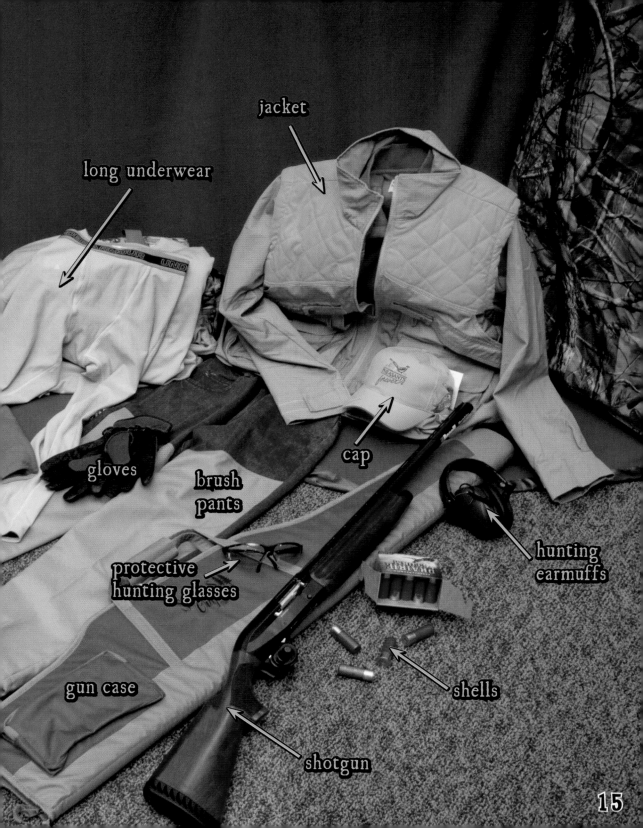

jacket

long underwear

cap

gloves

brush
pants

hunting
earmuffs

protective
hunting glasses

shells

gun case

shotgun

15

Chapter 3

Skills and Techniques

Many hunters use trained hunting dogs. Dogs follow scent trails to find pheasants. Dogs **flush** pheasants or point their heads toward them. Dogs also **retrieve** fallen pheasants.

flush—to force pheasants from their hiding places
retrieve—to bring back

Wild Fact:

Retrievers, setters, spaniels, and pointers are all popular pheasant hunting dogs.

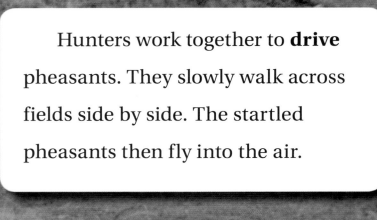

Hunters work together to **drive** pheasants. They slowly walk across fields side by side. The startled pheasants then fly into the air.

Wild Fact:

Pheasants usually travel on foot. They fly only short distances to find cover.

drive—to walk side by side across a field to find pheasants

Hunters raise their guns to their shoulders. They aim their gun **barrels** just ahead of the flying pheasants before firing. This action is called leading.

barrel—the long, tube-shaped part of a shotgun

Wild Fact:

Pheasants often nest in farm fields. Hunters must get permission to hunt on private farmland.

Chapter 4

Safety

Safe hunters treat all guns as if the guns are loaded. They keep guns unloaded until ready to use. They never lean loaded guns against trees, fences, or cars.

A detailed map and a compass help keep hunters on course.

Pheasant hunters shoot only at flying birds. They do not shoot low enough to hit a person or dog. They never point guns at dogs or other people.

Wild Fact:

Most states require safety classes for hunters born after a certain year.

Safe hunters protect their hearing from loud gunshots with earplugs or hunter's earmuffs. They may wear shooting glasses to shield their eyes from stray shot.

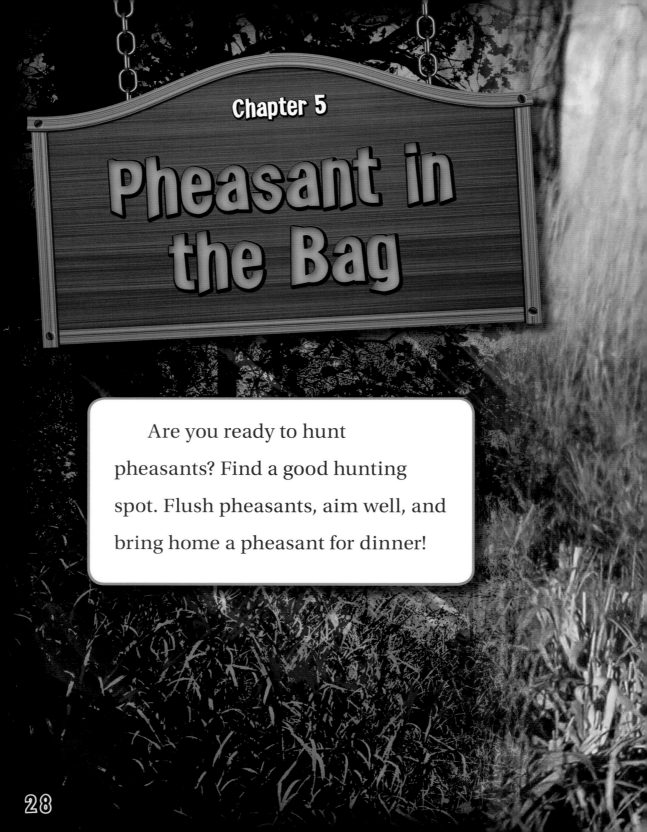

Chapter 5

Pheasant in the Bag

Are you ready to hunt pheasants? Find a good hunting spot. Flush pheasants, aim well, and bring home a pheasant for dinner!

Wild Fact:

Minnesota hunters formed Pheasants Forever in 1982. This group works to educate people and protect pheasant habitats.

Glossary

barrel (BAYR-uhl)—the long, tube-shaped metal part of a gun through which bullets or shot pellets travel

brush (BRUHSH)—a thick growth of shrubs and small trees close to the ground

compass (KUHM-puhs)—an instrument people use to find the direction in which they are traveling

drive (DRIVE)—a method of finding pheasants that involves a group of hunters walking side by side across a field

flush (FLUSH)—to force an animal or bird from its hiding place

habitat (HAB-uh-tat)—the place and natural conditions in which an animal lives

retrieve (ri-TREEV)—to bring something back

shot (SHOT)—small metal beads or pellets fired from a shotgun

Read More

Klein, Adam G. *Hunting.* Outdoor Adventure! Edina, Minn.: Abdo Pub. Co., 2008.

Martin, Michael. *Pheasant Hunting.* The Great Outdoors. Mankato, Minn.: Capstone Press, 2008.

Internet Sites

FactHound offers a safe, fun way to find Internet sites related to this book. All of the sites on FactHound have been researched by our staff.

Here's all you do:

Visit *www.facthound.com*

Type in this code: 9781429660051

Index